Acknowledgment
WALLIS, DR. CHARLES AND HARPER & ROW PUBLISHERS, INC., for "Prayer" by Gail
Brook Burket from The Treasure Chest. Copyright © 1965 by Dr. Charles Wallis.

God grant me Serenity

to accept the things
I cannot change
Courage
to change
the things
I can
and
Wisdom
to know
the difference

God grant me Serenity

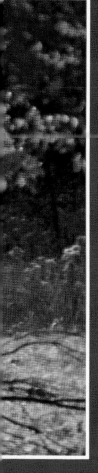

Therefore being justified by faith, we have peace with God through our Lord Jesus Christ: By whom also we have access by faith into this grace wherein we stand, and rejoice in hope of the glory of God.

Romans 5:1-2

I know not by what methods rare,
But this I know: God answers prayer.
I know not if the blessing sought
Will come in just the guise I thought.
I leave my prayer to Him alone
Whose will is wiser than my own.

Eliza M. Hickok

This is the day which the Lord hath made; we will rejoice and be glad in it.

Psalm 118:24

Take therefore no thought for the morrow: for the morrow shall take thought for the things of itself.

Matthew 6:34

Trust in the Lord, and do good; so shalt thou dwell in the land, and verily thou shalt be fed.

Delight thyself also in the Lord; and he shall give thee the desires of thine heart.

Commit thy way unto the Lord; trust also in him; and he shall bring it to pass.

Psalm 37:3-5

Serenity

God grant me Serenity to accept the things I cannot change

And the peace of God, which passeth
all understanding, shall keep your
hearts and minds through Christ Jesus.

Philippians 4:7

Let us learn to be content with what we
have.
Let us get rid of our false estimates, set
up all the higher ideals—
    a quiet home,
    vines of our own planting,
    a few books full of the inspiration of
      genius,
    a few friends worthy of being loved
      and able to love in return,
    a hundred innocent pleasures that
      bring no pain or remorse,
    a devotion to the right that will
      never swerve,
    a simple Christianity empty of all
      bigotry, full of trust and hope and
      love—
and to such a philosophy this world
will give up all the joy it has.

David Swing

Now the God of hope fill you with all joy and peace in believing, that ye may abound in hope, through the power of the Holy Ghost.

Romans 15:13

Wherefore we receiving a kingdom which cannot be moved, let us have grace, whereby we may serve God acceptably with reverence and godly fear.

Hebrews 12:28

Let the words of my mouth, and the meditation of my heart, be acceptable in thy sight, O Lord, my strength, and my redeemer.

Psalm 19:14

Serenity

God grant me
Courage to change the
things I can

I know both how to be abased, and I know how to abound: every where and in all things I am instructed both to be full and to be hungry, both to abound and to suffer need. I can do all things through Christ which strengtheneth me.

Philippians 4:12-13

Low I kneel through the night again,
    Hear my prayer, if my prayer be
right!
Take for Thy token my proud heart broken.
    God, guide my arm! I go back to the fight.

Anonymous

For with God nothing shall be impossible.

Luke 1:37

I do not ask to walk smooth paths
Nor bear an easy load.
I pray for strength and fortitude
To climb the rock-strewn road.

Give me such courage I can scale
The hardest peaks alone,
And transform every stumbling block
Into a steppingstone.

Gail Brook Burket

But they that wait upon the Lord shall
renew their strength; they shall mount
up with wings as eagles; they shall run,
and not be weary; and they shall walk,
and not faint.

Isaiah 40:31

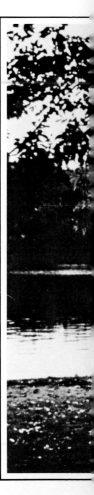

Courage

Courage

That ye might walk worthy of the Lord unto all pleasing, being fruitful in every good work, and increasing in the knowledge of God; Strengthened with all might, according to his glorious power, unto all patience and longsuffering with joyfulness.

Colossians 1:10, 11

For I am persuaded, that neither death, nor life, nor angels, nor principalities, nor powers, nor things present, nor things to come, Nor height, nor depth, nor any other creature, shall be able to separate us from the love of God, which is in Christ Jesus our Lord.

Romans 8:38-39

Lord, let me give and sing and sow
    And do my best, though I
In years to come may never know
    What soul was helped thereby.

Content to feel that thou canst bless
    All things however small
To someone's lasting happiness
    So, Lord, accept my all.

Prudence Tasker Olsen

I have glorified thee on the earth: I
have finished the work which thou
gavest me to do. I have manifested thy
name unto the men which thou gavest
me out of the world: thine they were,
and thou gavest them me; and they
have kept thy word. I pray for them: I
pray not for the world, but for them
which thou hast given me; for they are
thine.

John 17:4,6,9

Courage

God grant me Wisdom to know the difference

Teach me, O Lord, the way of thy
statutes; and I shall keep it unto the
end. Give me understanding, and I
shall keep thy law; yea, I shall observe
it with my whole heart. Make me to go
in the path of thy commandments; for
therein do I delight. Incline my heart
unto thy testimonies, and not to
covetousness. Turn away mine eyes
from beholding vanity; and quicken
thou me in thy way. Stablish thy word
unto thy servant, who is devoted to thy
fear. Turn away my reproach which I
fear: for thy judgments are good.
Behold, I have longed after thy
precepts: quicken me in thy
righteousness.

Psalm 119:33-40

For God giveth to a man that is good in
his sight wisdom, and knowledge, and
joy.

Ecclesiastes 2:26

One of the hardest lessons we have to learn in this life, and one that many persons never learn, is to see the divine, the celestial, the pure in the common, the near at hand,—to see that heaven lies about us here in this world.

John Burroughs

For the Lord giveth wisdom: out of his mouth cometh knowledge and understanding. He layeth up sound wisdom for the righteous: he is a buckler to them that walk uprightly.

Proverbs 2:6-7

When God lights the soul with wisdom, it floods the faculties, and that man knows more than ever could be taught him.

Meister Eckhart

Wisdom

Wisdom

Almighty God, the Giver of Wisdom, . . . enable me, if it be Thy will, to attain knowledge . . . and grant that I may use that knowledge which I shall attain, to Thy glory.

Samuel Johnson

Give me now wisdom and knowledge, that I may go out and come in before this people: for who can judge this thy people, that is so great? And God said to Solomon, Because this was in thine heart, and thou hast not asked riches, wealth, or honour, nor the life of thine enemies, neither yet hast asked long life; but hast asked wisdom and knowledge for thyself, that thou mayest judge my people, over whom I have made thee king: Wisdom and knowledge is granted unto thee.

2 Chronicles 1:10-12

God · grant me
Serenity
to accept the things
I cannot change
Courage to change
the things
I can
Wisdom and
to know
the difference

Selected by Gladys Pucillo
Designed by Bonnie Weber
Calligraphy by Maurianna Nolan

PHOTO CREDITS

Robert Grana—pp.4,5; Robert E. Lee—pp.6,7;
Maria Demarest—pp.8,9; Ed Cooper—pp.10,11;
Jeff Munk—pp.12,13,18,19; Doris G. Barker—
pp.14,15; Jim Patrick—pp.16,17,20,21; Bruce
Ando—pp.22,23; Carl Moreus—pp. 24,25; Pete
Haynes—pp.26,27; Jay Johnson—pp.28,29.